Mental Graffiti

The Collected Random Thoughts From A Creative Mind

Mental Graffiti

The Collected Random Thoughts From A Creative Mind

Scott E. Pond

DARKER REALITY
DRS
STUDIOS

This is a work of fiction. Names, characters, places, and incidents either are the product of the author's imagination or used fictitiously. Any resemblance to actual persons, living or dead, events, or locales is entirely coincidental.

Copyright © 2021 by Scott E. Pond. All rights reserved.
Published in the United States of America ('Merica!)
by Darker Reality Studios
http://DarkerReality.com

Photography by Bruce Press Photography
(**http://brucefpressphotography.com**)

Cover design, cover art, interior illustrations, and book design by Scott E. Pond Designs, LLC (**http://scottpond.com**)

Edited and proofed by Tori Duke Pond, Lisa-Anne Samuels Moore, Sue Baiman, and Val Griswold-Ford

Dung Beetle illustration
by Arthur Wright (aka Noble Bear, **https://noblebearaw.wordpress.com/**)

Ponderine illustration
by Marc Lapierre (**https://marctoons.carbonmade.com/**)

Stock photography by 123RF (**http://123RF.com**)

Library of Congress Cataloging-in-Publication Data

Pond, Scott E
 Mental Graffiti / Scott E Pond—1st ed.
 p. cm.
 1. Humor—General. 2. Humor—Anecdotes & Quotations.
 3. Humor—Puns & Word Play. 4. Humor—Adult.
 5. Fiction—Humorous/General. 6. Fiction—Humorous/Black Humor.
 I. Pond, Scott. II. Title

Library of Congress Control Number: 2015920777
Print ISBN: 978-1-944672-00-3
eBook ISBN: 978-1-944672-01-0

PRINTED IN THE UNITED STATES OF AMERICA
11 10 9 8 7 6 5 4 3 2

SECOND EDITION: Second Printing—January 2021

Do you want to hear news and get an email when Scott publishes a new book or has a new project being released? Go to his website and sign up for Scott's newsletter today!

Visit and subscribe: **http://scottpond.com/**

The only time you'll receive emails is when he has new published books or new projects being released (and no more frequently than once a month!).

Also, you will not get spammed!

He doesn't even like spam... too much sodium.

For my Dad, Stanley Pond:
You taught me to find meaning in all aspects of life,
to cut my losses and take a different path when I should,
and inspired me to always do better the next time.
I miss you, more every day. Fly high, buddy.

ACKNOWLEDGEMENTS

As with raising children, it takes a village to conceive, create, and publish a book. [Ok, maybe not a good example... it actually takes an egg and sperm to conceive a human child. If it was actually a village doing the conceiving, that would be one creepy orgy. Dammit, I hate analogies. They never really work, you know? However, stay with me on this one... it'll make sense. Maybe.]

If not for the following people, you would not be holding this book (either electronically or in dead-tree format) in your greedy little hands. These folks are my backbone and my port in any storm.

Tori Duke Pond—For being my rock in the continuous storm of life, the center of my multi-verse, and, like, my bestest most goodest most grooviest friend, like evah. I couldn't do anything without you and wouldn't want to. Thank you for correcting my knuckle-headedness... it's pretty much a full-time job in and of itself. Thank you for finally finding me.

Jan Pond—For being my mother when I truly needed one. You've done more for me than you will ever know. I love you, mom.

Logan and Rachael Pond—For being fantastic children and a constant reminder that I make really good stuff. I mean seriously, just look at you two.

Scott Sigler and AB Kovacs—For starting me back down the creative path, which led (somehow) to this. Thank you for your friendship, trust, and creative synergy. Some debts can never be repaid. I owe you.

Paul E. Cooley—For continually reminding me that anyone can do this, but that not everyone *should*. Thank you for helping me round out my skills and prompting me to push myself further. But more importantly, thank you for being such a great friend. Now, get back to your own writing!

Matt Wallace—For being my brother from another mother and mainly for your unspoken advice that to make it in this biz you need to be a boisterous mother f*cker with a punk rock tenacity and solid style.

Bruce Press—For forging ahead and taking the lead in forming your own creative career path. You and your photography are an inspiration.

Lisa-Anne Samuels Moore—For your invaluable editing, advice, insight, experience, insomnia improv writing therapy, and friendship.

Sue Baiman—For your editing acumen, friendship, and impeccable timing with blunt, constructive criticism.

Val Griswold-Ford—For kicking my ass and getting me up to the art studio for some much-needed creative inspiration, along with your fabulous final proofreading skills, friendship, and literary vision.

Charlie Brown—For your word-slinging back copy mojo. You are one groovy, smooth cat and more awesome than a boom-stick.

Pondy's Street Samurai—For promoting this, along with all the others. You make this stuff look easy (when in reality, it is far from it). You are all fabulous and at least a couple of you are gorgeous:

Jason Banks; Gordy Barker; Lulu Bizou; Beth Copenhaver; Seth Davis; Tori Duke; Paul Ellis; Melody Emerson; A. F. Grappin; Val Griswold-Ford; JP Harvey; Danny Lundy; Kimberly McCloe; Alan "Wolf" Roark; Dave Robison; Allen Sale; David Sobkowiak; Kenttrell Trotter; John Walker; and Katharina Winter

My Alpha Squad—For helping me whittle down the list to something more manageable, I owe the following a debt (to be paid in frosty brews or other acceptable forms of acceptable bribery):

Jennifer Burtt; Peter O'Malley; Delio Niro; Steven Ort; Crystal Pond; Julie Press; Alan "Wolf" Roark; Andrew Ryan; and John "BigJohn" Vizcarra

There are so many others (authors, fellow creatives, friends, family, and even my poo-eating rotten arch-enemies) who have contributed to the motivation to make this a reality: you may or may not know who you are, but know that I know who you are.

Thank you, everyone, for all that you do.

Don't. Ever. Stop.

Scott E. Pond

AUTHOR'S NOTE

My brand of humor tends to be a little too high brow for the average person to intellectually process. It must be my rampant use of political and societal themes, not to mention my revolutionary insight.

Or maybe it's just my consistent use of poop, vagina, STD, and penis jokes.

I seem to have always had a sense of humor that has been deemed "quirky" by some, "weird" by others, "inspired" by a couple enlightened individuals, and downright "dirty" by a select few [those few who wouldn't know something was funny if it slapped them in the face]. The problem was, until the last decade or so, I really didn't show it that much (in my opinion). Or at least I don't think so. I'm sure if you asked my old school friends or old navy chums they would tell you differently.

But from my recollection, I was downright quiet.

To be honest, it hasn't been until this latter part of my life that I've finally gained the confidence (and started not giving a crap about what people think about me) to actually speak (or in this case, write) the whimsical things that pop into my head. Until recently, at least, I haven't exactly been brimming with self-conviction.

Why, you may ask? Why this lack of confidence? Hmmm?

Believe it or not—and most folks who know me today, speak with me today, certainly will *not* believe it—it all stems from my early childhood. It actually extends beyond that, but it all *started* in my early childhood.

You see, not only was I a hefty child (read: fat) but I also had (had being the operative keyword) a debilitating speech impediment. I was a stutterer. No, really, it's true! Still am technically, but more then. Not a once in a while stutterer, mind you. No siree. Those folks are what I call "functional stutterers." I was what I call a "non-functional stutterer." But what is a non-functional stutterer? Think Mel Tillis, but about x3 times worse. (If you don't know who Mel Tillis is, he was an old-school country-music singer. Singed beautifully but when he talked, total stutterer. Do a YouTube search for "Mel Tillis Interview" and check out his level of stuttering to get a feel).

My stuttering and stammering was so bad I was lucky to say two or three words before getting hung up or jack-hammering the word. It was so bad that the school administration back then were considering to put me in the "special education" classes because, in their opinion (read: "extreme ignorance"), they viewed it as a "learning disability" (when in fact it was more of a "communication disability," but I digress). It was so bad that when the administration finally got their collective heads out of their backsides and hired a professional for myself and several other students, I ended up spending 7+ years in speech therapy just to get to the point of being a "functional" stutterer.

[For a functional stutterer example, think Stuttering John from the Howard Stern Show (look him up if you have to).]

This in itself was bad enough.

But imagine being a stuttering fat kid.

Among other children... among asshole children.

"Hey, look, it's F-f-f-f-f-at Man! Talk to us Fat Man! Oh, you can't, because you are a piece of shit retard. Hey retard! Can you hear me! S-s-s-say something, you f*cking s-s-s-stuttering dummy!"

Lovely, huh?

That's just an example of the mildest form of bullshit that I went through as a kid, along with the physical bullying.

Apparently, it is high sport to punch, pinch, spit on, and knock down stuttering fat kids. Who knew?

Great times, man, great times.

Well, somehow I managed to survive it all. Not fully intact, mind you, but at least to a level that was recoverable.

Needless to say, that shit leaves its mark on a person. A mark that manifested itself mainly in confidence issues and social anxiety, which took years to dig myself out of. But dammit, I finally did.

But how did I survive?

Honestly, through my art and my sense of humor.

My art allowed me to communicate my thoughts, feelings, and huge concepts visually, a skill that has kept me in good stead for a long time. My art was my refuge when times got really rough. It was also one of the ways, sometimes, that

I was able to connect with people. Still does to a large extent. I've been able to meet a lot of fantastic creative people through my artwork. Visual mediums are great in this regard.

However, my humor is the one piece of verbal communication that I was always able to use, even if I had to stammer it out painfully. One liners, quips, short jokes... these have been a staple of my verbal communication throughout my life.

Why?

Because I could belt them out quickly, with minimal interference (mostly) from my speech impediment. When I couldn't participate in long, drawn-out verbal discussions with my friends, I could at least throw out a quick comedic salvo to ensure I was still part of the conversation.

Being a part of it.

That was so critical, man. So critical in *feeling* connected, even if the tornado of thoughts and ideas in my head was mostly stuck there. It allowed me to feel part of everyone around me.

And, hey, if it also allowed me to be the center of attention for even a moment and, most importantly, have people laugh WITH me instead of AT me, then even more perfect. You have no idea how important the differentiation between those two words are. They mean the world to some people. Myself included.

Fast forward many years.

I now have kicked my speech impediment (mostly) and my confidence issues. Most people who I tell of my past are shocked and, I'm pretty sure, don't even believe me. Why would they when they never saw the struggle?

It does seem rather improbable and distant now. These days, I speak at length with much vociferous pontification (meaning: I speak a lot to a lot of people). Without stuttering.

Mostly.

But what about my humor?

Oh yeah, my humor is still there. It flows from just about everything I do, from everywhere, and almost all the time.

In fact, it has infected my social media presence since the first day I jumped into that maelstrom feet first. Social media is the place where I've been able to let down my comedic hair (*snicker*).

Without those public social media outlets, this book would never have been possible. You hold in your hands (either in dead-tree or digital) around six years worth of collected bits of humor. Mostly from my social media feeds. Some are brand-new and just materialized, inspired on the spot by the simple act of pulling this work together.

So here it is. Uncut and with a glistening, smooth shine, for your impeccable reading pleasure.

Just like a great penis joke.

Enjoy!

Scott E. Pond
Derry, New Hampshire
November 25, 2015

P.S. What the hell happened over the last five years? A pandemic? An attempted coup? I thought shit was crazy before… even my imagination wasn't up to task when it came to predicting what would have happened since the first printing of this book. Stay Safe, my friends, and look out for each other.

Scott E. Pond
Charlottesville, Virginia
January 6, 2021

FORWARD

We live in a world of instant news, instant thoughts, and instant outrage. Social media has provided civilization with a new means to misunderstand one another. It has proven our foolishness time and time again by spurring indignation over false information, and confusing the hell out of lots of people. Some individuals, known as "trolls," use social media to incite these misunderstandings and cause pain. Some, like Scott Pond, instead use it to elicit joy through humor and sarcasm.

Rather than troll people, Scott trolls life.

The human mind is a vessel chock-full of nonsense and relatively meaningless perceptions. Some of us turn that nonsense into smiles and laughter, occasionally punctuated with the angst we all feel over shared experiences like travel delays, traffic, and long hours at the workplace. And some humans absolutely excel at this.

Mental Graffiti is an assortment of social media posts from an often sleep-deprived artist and author. Much like his fantastic artwork and designs, Scott's off-the-wall observations, fictional anecdotes, and tongue-in-cheek social criticisms are a delight. Although he is frequently quiet in public, the words in this tome reveal a brain that is constantly talking, arguing with itself, and in desperate need of a long-assed vacation, preferably involving insomnia-free nights.

In a way, I hope that brain doesn't get this rest.

Scott's creations and missives are an absolute delight and I for one am willing to sacrifice his rest for my amusement. Not really, but it sounded like something he'd say off the cuff.

So while we consume the public thoughts he shares in real time, one wonders how long that brain has been turning the words around and around until they make sense.

Maybe that's why he doesn't sleep.

While he and I relentlessly trade barbs in public, dueling with words and inside jokes, he is a fellow-creator, a good friend, and a fantastic human being.

Don't let his goofiness make you think anything else.

In the spirit of full disclosure, I must admit that Mr. Pond is my cover designer and an invaluable resource for my writing and publishing efforts. That said, he's earned my trust again and again, and his friendship is one of the greatest boons of my career.

I look forward to everything he posts and every email he sends. On my worst days, Scott is dropping pun-filled gold that forces me to smile. I'm certain others feel the same way. *Mental Graffiti* is far too concise a volume, and often misses the context that created these observations. But that doesn't matter. The whimsy and calculated word play is a joy I'm glad he shares with us pedestrian humans on a daily (sometimes hourly) basis.

So while Scott Pond empties his brain's inner workings on to the page in snippets that are equal part humor and sarcasm, the rest of us are grinning like fools while we soak in his genius. *Mental Graffiti* will make you smile, laugh in disgust, or make you wonder what the hell he was thinking about when he put the words together.

We may never know. And perhaps that's just as well.

The mystery is part of their charm.

Paul E. Cooley

Author of The Black, The Street, Closet Treats, The Rider, *and the collected legends of* Garaaga

The Woodlands, Texas
November 27, 2015

Mental Graffiti

Life is like a butterfly... and other stupid metaphors.

An Orgasm: as close as you can get to heaven without actually dying. Hopefully. But what a way to go, eh?

Never have an affair with a ninja's wife.

I'm as jittery as a cat in a mouse factory.

I didn't realize there were four Mondays and one Friday this week.

Always, always, always:
read the small print.

_{By reading this text you have agreed to trade your soul to me for a bag of stale M&Ms.}

Just call me the Grand Poobah of Slinging Crap and Making It Sound Groovy (GPoSCaMISG)!

In a quandary and need your help. Trying to determine what kind of attitude I should have. Here's the choices: (1) take a serious, no-nonsense approach, (2) be sarcastic and humorous, or (3) have a short fuse and a "don't f*ck with me cause I could stab you at any minute" attitude. Trying to coordinate my attire with my demeanor.

I had a very strange dream last night involving robotic assassin midgets on unicorns, waving bright pink plastic sporks and singing oompa-loompa songs; all while hunting field mice wearing riding chaps. I blame the late-night spicy tacos and the telepathic influence of Steven Spielberg.

A BJ: As far as jobs go, that one really sucks.

Coffee: The breakfast of champions... and those avoiding real food due to hangovers.

May the beer be with you. Always.

If you try to fail, and succeed, which have you done?

This is for all you Moms out there - Mornings: ruining a good night's sleep for forever.

If everything tastes like chicken, what the heck does chicken taste like? I bet it tastes like human.

Catch on fire with enthusiasm and people will come for miles to watch you burn. Burn, baby, burn...

I wish I had a super power. Something like the ability to fling boogies with pinpoint accuracy. Or fabric x-ray vision. I'm not really picky.

It's so windy here that I think I just saw Auntie Em fly by in her rocking chair... or maybe it was that mean old Miss Almira Gulch on her bicycle. Did anyone see a small yipping dog?

PETA: People for Eating Tasty Animals... yum!

Mental Graffiti **33**

- Head Cheese
- Chuck
- Fore Shank
- Rib
- Short Loin
- Sirloin
- Round
- Brisket
- Short Plate
- Flank
- Sweet Meats
- Round

If we aren't supposed to eat animals, why are they made of meat and taste so yummy?

I'm getting really tired of people who are about as consistent as an old, worn D100 dice roll.

There is nothing quite like waking up with sharp back pain. Makes you all at once realize that you are alive. Then, a few minutes later, you start to reap the benefits of nerves and consciousness. Unfortunately.

Fun Quote From Human Sexuality Class: "In this class, we want to use the official terms for things—such as "penis," "vagina," "testicles," "breasts," "anus," "sphincter," and "Sexually Transmitted Infections, or STIs." Terms, such as "golden marble bag of fun," "elephant snout," "fun globes," "balloon knot," and "sweater puppies," while colorful, may be open to misinterpretation, and should not be used."

Wait a minute! Aren't humans also made out of meat? Now I have a potential moral dilemma.

I know. I'll answer all Cs. I should get at least 25%. Right?

An assignment from Human Sexuality class: bring in an item that reminds you of "sex." What the heck am I supposed to bring??? Can't exactly bring in my pet love-sheep, the dungeon racks, or the assless chaps... So what can I bring in...?

There is a BIG difference between appreciating the natural assets of the desired sex and just being a sexist asshole. DUH.

As I always say (as of today): most think I'm either interestingly gorgeous or gorgeously interesting. According to some, I'm both. According to others, I'm neither. Narrow-minded fools.

My bed is whining about being lonely, so I guess I should head there and dive into dreamland. Tonight, I'm hoping for a nice, low-key, flying, super-agent dream. That would be nice. But if there is even a single robotic assassin midget again, I'm not gonna be a very unhappy camper! Got me, Spielberg?

I challenge anyone to name anything that is better than munching on an Oreo freshly dipped in ice-cold milk.

Mowing the Lawn: Now just to pick the proper lawn mowing ensemble. What do you think? Should I go with the Daisy Duke shorts and halter-top? Or should I go topless with just a thong? What would cause the most mental trauma to the neighbors and make Miley proud?

I like cheese.

Mowing the Lawn: I finally finished mowing the front yard. After all our fashion discussions, I chose to forgo wearing the halter top, thong, tiara, flip-flops and the goggles. Instead, I decided to go buck-ass naked with just a pair of hiking boots and earmuffs. Pictures will be $50 a piece, $100 if I can call it art.

"Long drive again?"
"Yes, unfortunately."
"Bored?"
"Yes."
"At least you have yourself to talk to, so we won't be hurting for intelligent dialogue."
"Very true. We're so smart and interesting."

Things I Am (NOT) Thankful For (#01): Fox prematurely canceling every single good show they ever pilot. And by every good show, I mean "Firefly."

Ever notice that it gets dark just before it's time for bed? That's pretty convenient, isn't it?

They say there comes a time in everyone's life when they just HAVE to dance. My day is probably coming. No one is looking forward to that day.

Oh, sweet nectar of the gods,

Why doth thee burn me lips?

Thoust art a bitter god.

Wretched liquid of life,

I forever curse thee,

Bear thy name as a warning.

I name thee coffee.

Good night, my peeps. This tired old man is off to bed. I'll have a nice dream about each of you. This time I'll make sure the dream-clothing stays on and that there are no trampolines, hand-cuffs, ponies, feathers, or pudding. Really, I promise.

Post Lunch Food Coma Battle: Why oh why won't 5PM just stop playing games and get here already?

Man, I'm friggin' hot. Blame genetics.

Birthday: Greetings and salutations, earthling, on the commemoration of your successful navigation out of the birth canal. We give you a reprieve from abduction and probing on this day.

One more hour of work. Give me the strength today not to put someone out of my misery in that last hour.

I wish I was made of fine, soft Corinthian Leather; that way Ricardo Montalbán could extol my virtues in stylish commercials.

Seen at the Laundromat: PLEASE REMOVE ALL YOUR CLOTHING WHEN THE LIGHT GOES OUT. That's a little dangerous in public, isn't it? But okay, if you insist.

Being a teacher would be so much more enjoyable if there were no such thing as students. Or senior faculty staff.

Don't look now but I'm naked... under my clothes.

Ever notice that no matter how many times you pick a wedgy, there is always another to take its place? Conspiracy or coincidence?

I'm a gorgeous, witty, and awesome dude. Anyone who disagrees is just jealous.

Bed Time: Do you hear it? It sounds like?... Could it be?... Yes!... It sounds like the promise of a good night's sleep. I get to see if it's a good promise, or just another hollow promise revealed as that rat bastard, Insomnia.

It's Friday. Do you know
where your weekend is?

Shocked the physical therapist by being able to touch my toes properly. Apparently fat guys aren't supposed to be limber. Wait until she sees my trapeze act.

It's a scientific fact that men are way cooler when they are asleep. I think it's time for me to get really groovy!

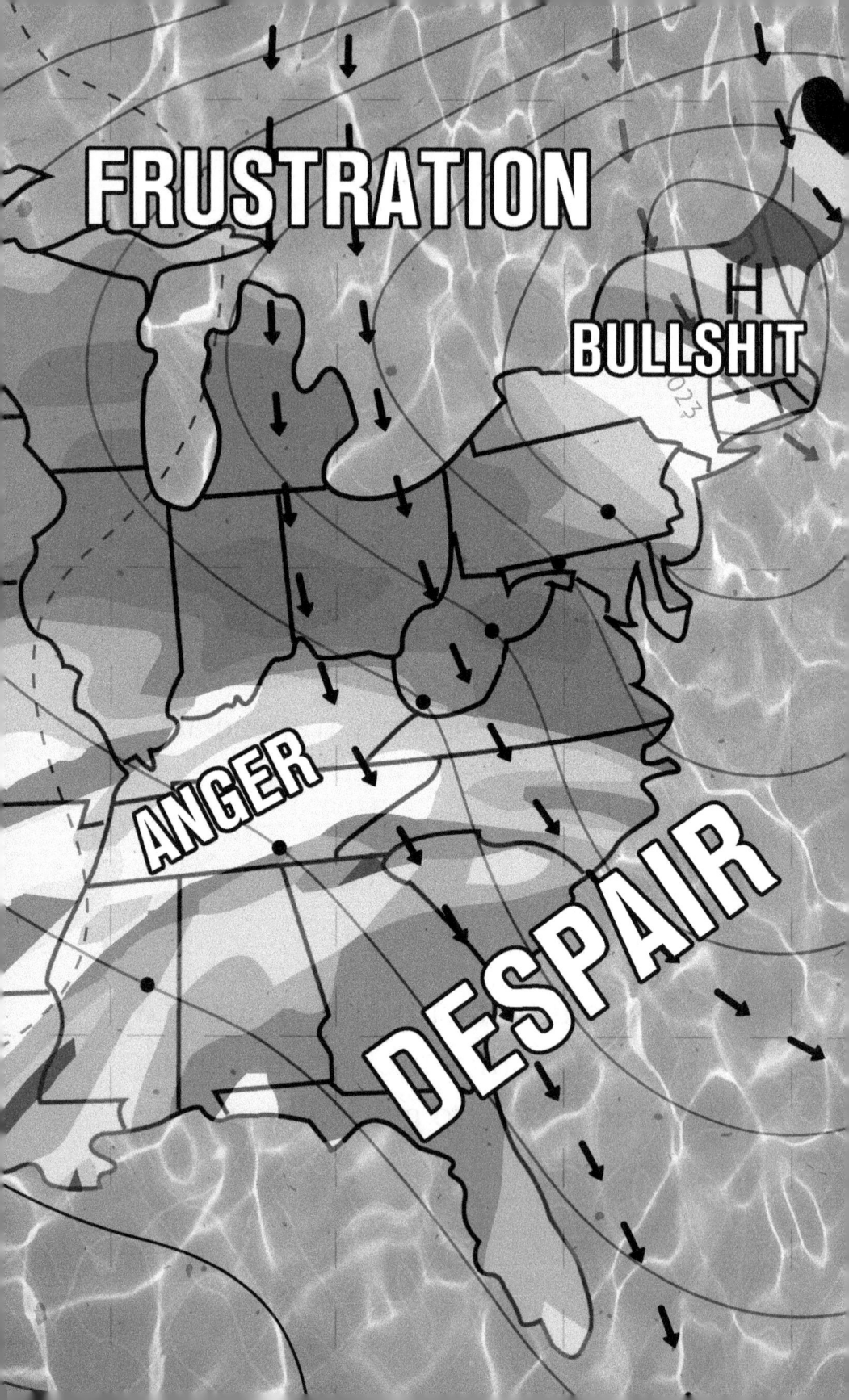

Workday Forecast: Heavy amounts of bullshit, gusts of despair and anger, and liberal periods of frustration throughout. Stay home today, folks; it's just not worth it.

"Poop or poop not, there is no try." #Number2MovieQuotes

I wonder if they make titanium toothpicks? The wooden ones keep snapping and splintering when I use them to try to prop my drooping eyelids open.

Rampant, selfish consumerism does not a happy person make.

Milk is the secret to winning any loogie contest.

Watched "Steel Magnolias" for the first time. I literally felt my estrogen levels increase and heard the screams of millions of testosterone molecules as they were obliterated.

Good morning, everyone. Last night I dreamed we all had the same dream. Did anyone else dream that?

Tired of being civilized. Thinking about going feral. Always wanted to run around dirty, naked, and growling. Without being drunk.

Looking forward to sucking the life, hope, and joy out of someone today. If you're lucky, it could be you.

That must have been some interesting mix of sex and drugs that brought us the Hokey Pokey. Wonder what specific chemical cocktail its creators were on so I can get some of their "inspiration."

The hamsters powering the Internet are exceptionally slow today.

On days like today I'm so thankful that Al Gore invented the internet and coffee. Now I'm just waiting for a brilliant mind to create an intravenous caffeine dispenser. Hurry it up, Al!

Well, HELLO, weekend! Wow, are you looking good or what!? I've been thinking about you all week. Let's get it on!
A Barry White song begins to play

You always know when you're getting close to home when you start seeing cars held together with Duct Tape. #PennsylTucky

Mondays should be boycotted due to lack of interest. Or at least due to a lack of motivation.

At the horse races. Decided not
to stay for the sacrificial slaying of
the slowest horse, though I hear
the glue ceremony is exquisite.

Kind of nice to start my morning
commute with a lovely rainbow.
Even though it reminds me of those
f*cking leprechauns. Selfish lucky
charm and gold hoarders. Why can't
those little bastards share their good
fortune, huh? Bunch of bullshit, I tell
ya. F*cking miniature assholes! But
anyway, it was a very pretty rainbow.

Things I Am (NOT) Thankful For (#02): Sauerkraut. Seriously, anything that is named after a bitter German should not be considered food. Nasty crap.

Dysentery: Mother Nature's perfect diet, exercise, and weight loss plan.

I'm, like, all cultured and shit, f*ckers.

Cruising Walmart for babes is like looking for Best Customer Service Award recipients at the DMV.

Dear lord, I didn't think this week would ever end. I've never been so grateful to be wrong.

After an afternoon of yard work I'm smelling like a real man and I'm wondering: why do "real men smell like sweaty, dirty hobos?"

It is hot today. Considering changing my name to S. Weaty Balzack.

Mowed the lawn today. No, that isn't a euphemism. Though I kind of wish it were.

I also trimmed the bush. Yes, that is a euphemism.

And now I begin my epic battle with the ALSD... the After Lunch Sleepy Daemons. The earth shall tremble. The heavens will... be... *yawn*... zzzzzzZZZ...

I know it's been rainy for a while, but the fact I'm growing gills has me a little concerned.

I've got a pocket, got a pocket full of sunshine. Oh, and lint.

It's a concrete jungle out there, folks.
Make sure you bring a jackhammer.

I can think of a dozen uses
for Vegemite. Not a single one
involves actual consumption.

You ever notice that the people who
keep flapping their mouths at work are
the same ones who get nothing done?

Some days I wish I was a pampered French kitty-cat. I really would love to walk around saying Les Meow and Le Purr. You know, without the weird looks.

Le sigh. Les grumble. La bitch. Du moan. <French Angst>

You know, hotel room coffee isn't too bad once you get past the taste of sweaty socks in your mouth. #HelloCaffeineMyFriend

Thank you,
oh Gods of Liquid Life,
for your gift of
wakefulness that has sustained
me this morning.
May your mocha-colored
ambrosia help me continue
through my afternoon
as I baste in your nectar
(with a bit of milk
and sugar, please)
and as I face your most evil foe:
The Daemon of Post-Lunch Drowsiness.

I need a bevy of beauties to pamper me for the rest of the day and tell me how manly I am. Send your applications to scott@scottpond.com

Remember: Knuckle-thumping melons for freshness or feeling for ripeness is okay at the supermarket. Not so much on a first date.

Time for bed. We're going to film a Telemundo episode in dreamland tonight and you're all invited. So, bring those wacky outfits. The more the better.

Bacon. #ThePerfectDaydream

Good morning, my friends. I know it's Monday, but try NOT to have a crappy day, will you? Remember: a crappy day means that the Mondays have won... and no one wants that!

The best part of making cookies: eating the raw dough and playing salmonella roulette.

What a beautiful day. It's a great day to strip naked, rub baby oil all over until you glisten, and take a stroll through town. Who's with me?

I think I need an alter ego. Not necessarily one to fight crime. Instead he would get to wear really snazzy outfits and post pictures of them on Instagram for no real reason. #YesISaidSnazzy

Friends don't let friends listen to ABBA while driving naked and drunk texting. #FriendlyServiceAnnouncement

BREAKING NEWS: Cats wake up New Hampshire man again and put their own lives in jeopardy. Also, 50 ways to prepare feline fritters. Full story at 11.

In the coming New Year, I resolve not to get angry at stupid people. I just wish there weren't so damn many of them.

Heading out to blow some snow. At this point, I think I'd almost rather be tossing some leaves.

Looking into the qualification process for becoming a garden gnome for the summer. I can stand around all day watching sun bathing beauties. It's a tough job but I can handle it.

There are days that I really don't feel like getting dressed to go to work. On the other hand, I really don't want to make people nauseous. #SoTorn

<Sings> The best part of waking up is a Long Island Iced Tea in your cup. (To hell with Folgers)

I wish every job made you wear flair. Big-ass buttons, suspenders, ascots, strings of beads, nipple rings... you know, the whole nine yards.

Boobs, beer, chocolate, and George Clooney. In case you need some motivation to face the day, just pick two of these and daydream about them. It'll help. Trust me.

Bed. It calls. Must obey. To disobey is to tempt the wrath of the sleep gods. Such is the fate of the sleepy.

Things I Am (NOT) Thankful For (#03): Rectal Exams at the doctors. Yes, I know that they are necessary in detecting certain types of issues; but they always make me feel like I've been sent to prison and assigned as a slap and tickle assistant to a huge black dude named Bubba. But I mean seriously, why do I need to have a weekly appointment for this and why does my Doc insist on call me "sweetheart" during it? It's just not right, I tell ya.

The projectile power of
Booze compels you!

Some day, when I grow up, I wouldn't mind being famous. Not "reality TV" famous, but more like someone who actually has a positive impact on society.

Well, HELLO, Friday! One of the most gorgeous days of the week! (Especially compared to Monday. Monday has BO and doesn't even have a nice personality. Monday is a real dog.).

When life hands you a bag of crap, don't fret. Just fertilize a garden.

I have a new goal in life: I'm going to bring back the widespread use of ascots. If it's good enough for Fred, it should be good for you.

Thinking about founding the International Order Of Dainty Silk Underwear Inspectors. Strictly for science, of course.

If there were any mystical or supernatural properties of "Sweat From A Fat Man," I could make a fortune selling vials of it.

I have successfully battled the Evil that is the grocery store, though the cost was high. Fare thee well, my lost green-back brothers.

Welcome to Toe-Puppet Thursday. Draw faces on your little piggies and hold a toe-puppet show for your boss today. It'll get you noticed.

Thank the Maker for coffee: the only thing strong enough to drag my lazy butt through this day.

I love going to Walmart because I get to see all the genetic missing-links between me and the slime my distant ancestors slithered out of.

Sleep, it calls me, luring me with promises of dream cheerleaders serving me dream beer. But I know its evil tricks. It really just wants to show me friggin' scary clowns... or Margaret Thatcher in a bikini!

Do unicorn steaks taste like Skittles or Lucky Charms' butt?

Work has totally slapped my ass and called me Sally. Calling it quits for the day and heading to the only place where I get some respect: my dreams.

I'm officially hanging up the cape for the week. Please contact the next superhero in line to fix your universe.

The toilets in public rest stops are prime examples of how disgusting and f*cked-up the average American is. I really miss manners and public decency.

You ever have one of those days when you'd rather crush some goblins and orcs and head out to the local tavern instead of facing the workday?

Toughest part about waking up and getting motivated in the morning is the waking up and getting motivated part.

Sticking one's toe in one's ear is much more difficult than it sounds. Even when naked and using an elaborate pulley system.

Is it the start of the zombie apocalypse if I see a bunch of dead people walking around? Or does it just mean it's Monday?

I would love to say it's gonna be a great day, but I just realized it's Monday. So I'm going to settle for not stabbing anyone and that will make it a great day.

I don't know why, but my internal dialog voice is always accompanied by a super fly techno beat. And it sings in Stevie Wonder's voice.

Wow! So this is what emerging
from a coma feels like.

Spiders! Finally! Something other
than clowns to be scared of!

I really wish I had a prehensile tail.

I must be healthy; my nose is cold and dry.

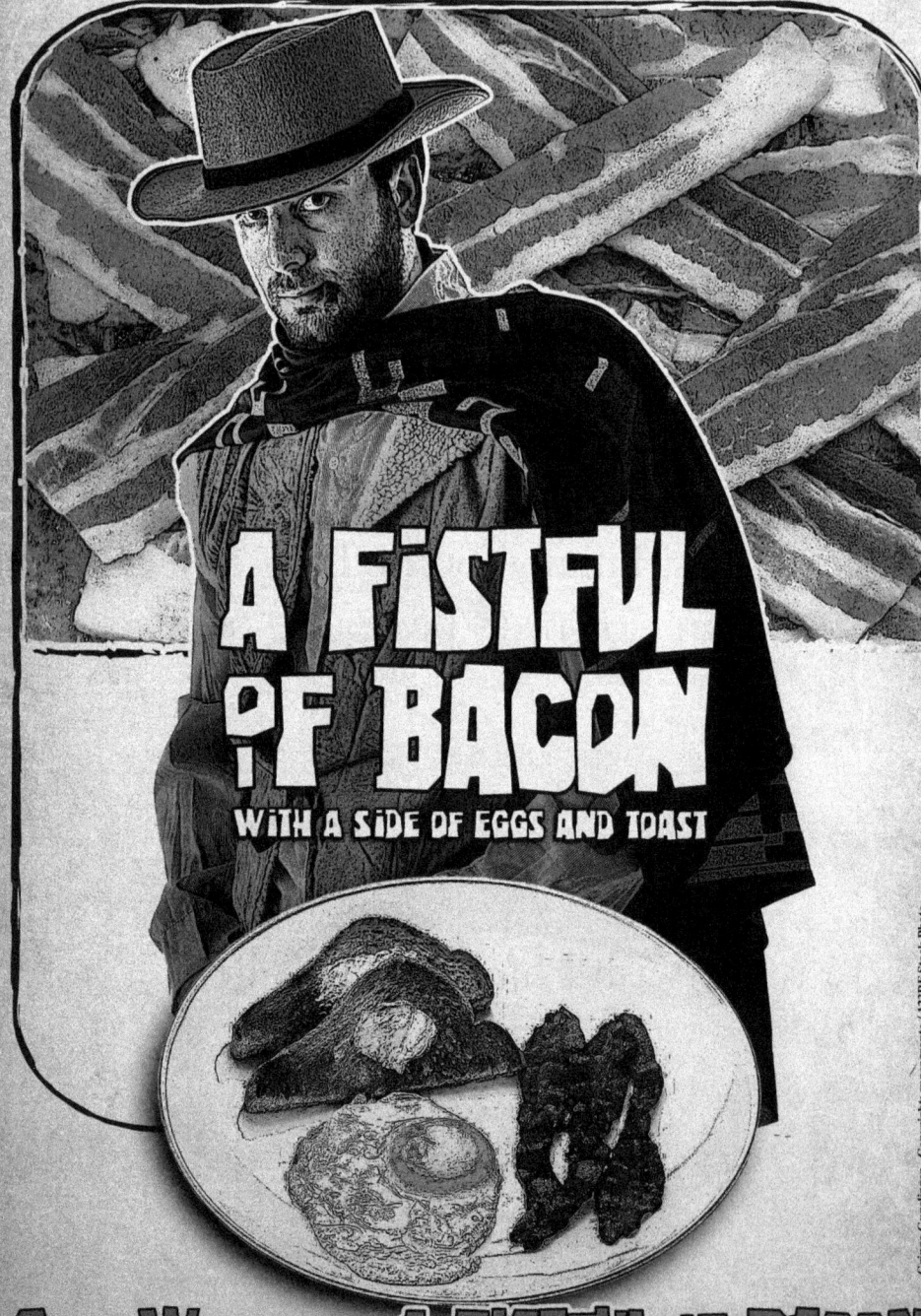

A Fistful of Bacon.
#BaconlisciousMovieTitles

Surely a little nap won't screw up my sleep tonight? #InfamousLastWords

San Francisco: Here, in a parallel universe, a Savior and a would-be King lost their lives. #Nocturnal

So, is it legally ok to roll a wino for some beer money? Also, does one really have to use that cash to purchase wine? I'm asking for a friend.

Thought of the Day: Stupidity should be painful. Bubonic-plague-just-kicked-in-the-nads level of painful.

There really should be more porn involving door to door sex sales people: <ding dong... door opens> "Hello sir/madam, can I interest you in a choreographed orgasm opportunity?"

I really hate hotels that are stingy with the extra pillows. How the hell am I supposed to make a pillow-fort with only 3 pillows?

It's time to put my trust again in the hands of pilots who are probably drunk and/or stoned.

Your ideal alter ego name = the first name of you favorite TV/movie character + your favorite normal/weird/exotic food. That makes me Captain Malcolm Vagina. And you?

Can we hurry up and get past these elections? I miss the news stories about smart people.

The voices are telling me I need to go to sleep. I don't know if I should listen to those voices or the ones telling me to go streaking.

I wish I could turn into a robotic cat and form a giant robot with a group of quirky friends to battle evil space monsters.

Well hello, Friday. Just between you and me: I'm going to be all over you like a fat dude at an all-you-can-eat buffet. Just saying.

Do people get a mandatory dipping in a mutagenic compound at age 70? Is that why they have to start going to the doctor so often? If not, how do you explain the fact that their ear lobes grow huge and that they're suddenly prehensile?

Not to brag or anything, but I'm having an Awesome Hair Day. #Bald

Things I Am (NOT) Thankful For (#04): F*cking Mondays. Seriously, why does every week have to start with a shitty day? You spend the week slaving away to get to the weekend. You have a nice relaxing weekend kicking your feet up and chilling. Then the first day of the workweek rolls around and BLAMO! Most weeks, it's like getting kicked in the rocks by a mule wearing high heels. And don't even get me started on the workweek. What f*cking sadomasochistic genius decided that we'd work five (count them, 5!) days and get two (a measly 2!) days off? WTF??? Why not work four days and have three days off? At least then it'd be somewhat even. Or hell, why not work three days and have four days off? We work hard, right? Grrrrrr. Screw you Monday, you're the cause of all this angst.

If the political commercials truthfully outed their candidate as selfish cheats, we could all get back to the real issue of who's hotter.

Caffeine, you totally failed me today. I thought you were better than that. I thought you were my friend! *sniffle*

Ok, remind me again: which candidate promised a lap dance for every American?

No matter how many times I try to drive with my eyes closed, some idiot always seems to honk the horn and scare me. Damn inconsiderate.

You will all need to speak up. I'm having a hard time hearing you all over the sound of how awesome I am.

I voterbated! (Dear lord, please don't let "voterbate" be something nasty done in a voting booth!)

Hello Hump Day. Please be gentle. It's my first time... <pause>... <snicker> naw, just joking. Ride me like a roller coaster. I can take it.

Not feeling witty is my equivalent of not feeling pretty. Today, I am bloated, ugly, and having a bad hair day. Don't look at me.

I think I just saw Bill Murray drive by in a pickup truck with a groundhog on his lap. Or was that yesterday? This ain't good.

SELLSY

Search for shit | Search | Sell on Sellsy | Register | Sign In

Clothing & Accessories | Jewelry | Bondage Accessories | Costume Play | Entertainment | Assassin Contracts | Baby Toys | "Companions"

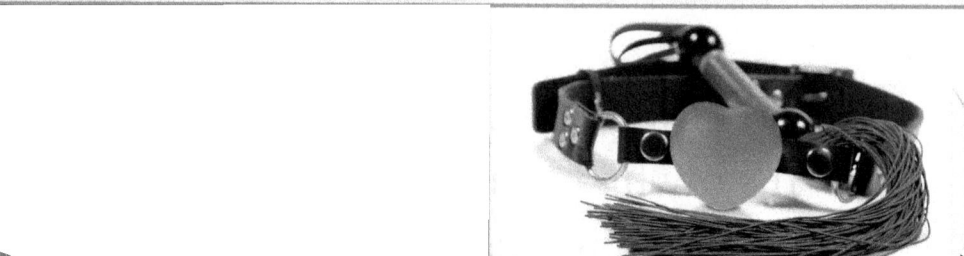

Adult Disciplinary Accessories

DISCOVER WEIRD-ASS SHIT YOU CAN'T FIND ANYWHERE ELSE

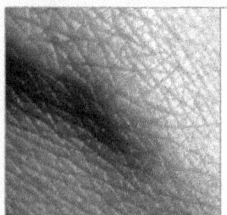

Editors Pick
Awesome Stuff Made From Human Skin

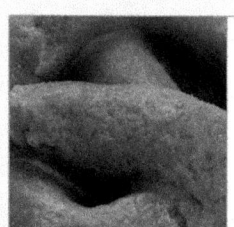

Editors Pick
High Quality and Classy Animal Feces Art

More Weird-Ass Shit

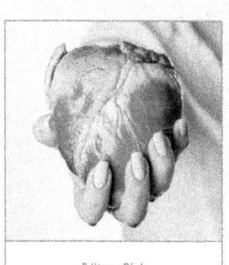

Editors Pick
Human Hearts and Kidneys (Bulk)

Editors Pick
Necomatic Spell Components

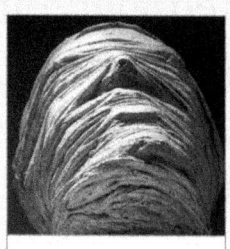

Editors Pick
Mummified Remains of Elvis

Editors Pick
Blood of Virgins

RECOMMENDATIONS FOR YOU
Based on the Freaky and Strange Crap You've Bought or Viewed

Weird Guy in a Cardboard Plane

Another Date with Balloon Bobby

Pancakes, Yummmmm

Pictures of Princess Puppy

"Dear god, your butt smells like a sewage plant. What did you eat???" [Things I want to yell out at that person exiting the rest room at work.]

I could've been a world class Sherpa.

I'm very surprised no one is selling crafts made out of human skin on Etsy. I think this might be an under-exploited market.

New Years Resolution #1: try
not to be so damn sexy

"Self" implies uniqueness and true individuality. In reality, we are just threads woven through the tapestry of causality, intertwined, both self and unity, with our fellow travelers on the entropic merry-go-round.

Chicken Fried Steak and Gravy:
the culinary world's answer
to prescription enemas.

For a Monday, I only feel a little violated. Thank god for chloroform.

Ever have one of those days?

Anyone know if I won an Oscar last night for my portrayal of an angst-ridden sexy artist in the Neil Simon production of I DON'T DO MONDAYS? My publicist isn't returning any of my 67 calls.

Had some grilled kangaroo for dinner tonight. How cool would it be if I could incorporate its genetic structure and grow a pouch overnight?

I wonder if I could do a revival of *Cats*, but as a monologue speaking in the voices of Heathcliff, Sylvester, and Garfield.

Whenever I have to pack for flights, I wish an 80s montage would start so I could do it a lot quicker.

FACT: You can't get your panties in a bunch if you don't wear any. SOLUTION: Go commando and lighten up.

Ever have one of those days when you really felt your primal roots and just wanted to fling your poo at someone?

When I grow up, I want to be a vintage pin-up model.

I'm holding a party in dreamland in about 15 minutes. Pop some Ambien and join the festivities. Just remember to BYODB (bring your own dream beer).

Was going to make some dinner; but then I asked myself, "what would my dentist want me to do?" So I'm now eating mint chocolate chip ice cream.

Caffeine, you again fail to drag me through the day. Instead you wine, dine, and dash. If I wasn't asleep, I'd feel violated and oh so unsatisfied.

Remember: if you must take a picture of me, my best side is my backside.

Flatulence: Nature's smelling salt.

Ever considered a life of crime smuggling black market NH maple syrup?

We are the hunters, gatherers, and foragers of our own happiness.

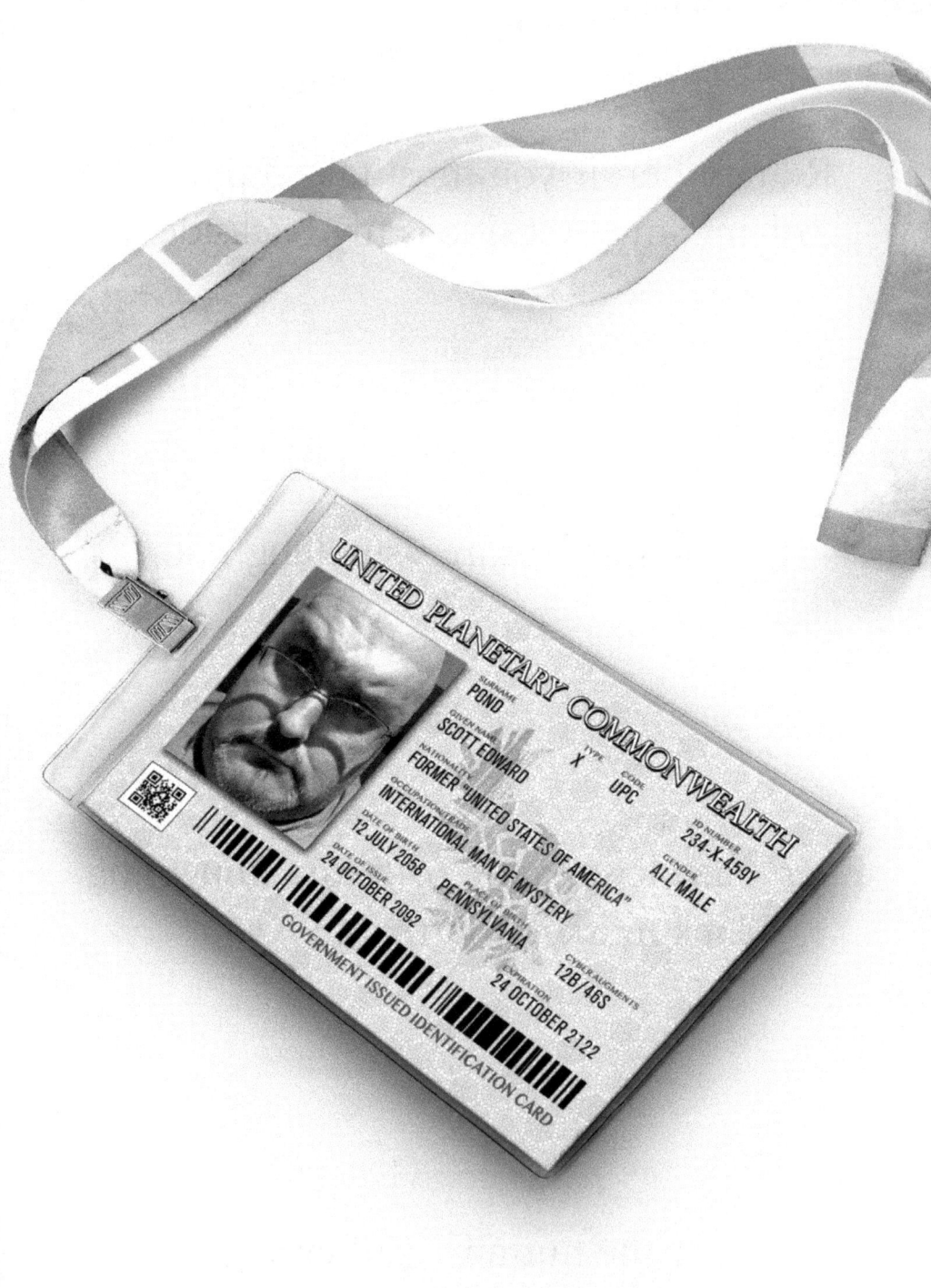

I think we should all plan on doing our best to have a fun day tomorrow. Me, I'm going to spend the day talking to everyone in the Swedish Chef's voice.

I'm thinking about forming an interpretive mariachi band.

I wonder if the passport folks will accept my occupation as "International Man of Mystery?"

Things I Am (NOT) Thankful For (#05): clowns, rats, zombies, hairy spiders, and Jay Leno's chin. These are the things that scare the crap out of me.

If my interpretive mariachi band doesn't pan out, my next genius idea is to open a combination art school and boarding house for wayward exotic dancers.

NKOTB (New Kids on the Block) should change their name to ODUTS (Old Dudes Up The Street)...

Happy Hump Day, my friends. Remember, it's also Hump Day for dogs, so protect your legs from their affections. #DamnHornyCanines

Dear Insomnia: I hate you almost as much as clown spiders. Sincerely, me.

I now know what my claim to fame will be: I'm going to bring parachute pants kicking and screaming back into fashion. Don't thank me. It's the least I could do.

Oh, no. I just realized my tramp stamp says, "Eat at Joe's" in kanji instead of "strength and respect."

Never wake up your significant other early unless it is for 1) food, 2) drink, 3) sex, 4) because they are late for an event, or 5) a natural disaster of biblical proportions is occurring/about to occur, upon pain of death. If you can somehow coordinate at least 2 of the above, you greatly increase your changes for survivability.

Well played, bacon. Well played, indeed. <slow 80's clap>

Observation: there really aren't enough songs about the therapeutic benefits of a good #2.

It is so difficult to be this sexy. You bland people don't know how easy you have it.

Be warned, Montezuma: I
too will get my revenge!

I really wish they made adult superhero
Underoos. I want to walk around
the block in a pair of Batman 'Roos
and strike fear into the neighbors.

Just like with Shakira, my hips don't lie.
I cannot, however, vouch for my knees.

I need a heavy metal guitarist to follow me around and play my theme song whenever I enter a room. On a related topic, I need a theme song.

So, while the attire of choice in Walmart is pajamas, apparently it is tracksuits at CVS.

I have successfully navigated yet another day without giving into the urge to clean up the gene pool through excessive violence. I'm sorry, folk, maybe tomorrow.

I really need to create my own monster out of spare human parts. I will call him George.

I hate getting older. Flashing my moob cleavage just doesn't open as many doors as it used to.

Please, feel free to ask me about my love of cheese.

But, Mom! I want to be a mindless follower with no aspirations, just like Billy!

All creatives have a muse. I just fear that mine is a one-armed cigar-smoking biker-transvestite with a lisp named Steyphan Honeybuns.

Had some Chinese for lunch today. God, I hope they aren't missed.

It's midnight. Do you know where your monkey is?

Last night's insomnia is today's narcolepsy.

I wonder if folks who handcraft mirrors get 7 years of good luck for each unit produced?

I could totally kick some ass in a break dancing battle with my signature "worm spasm" move.

I would love to have an alpaca or a camel as a pet. Any creature I can train to hock loogies at my enemies is a-ok in my book.

Move over caffeine: I think I'll upgrade to a pure adrenaline shot to the heart.

I am totally naked under these clothes.
You're welcome. BTW, we have brain
bleach for sale in the gift shop.

Dear Friday, I've missed you.
Don't ever go away and leave me
for so long again. Love, me.

If there is anything more bone-achingly
physically satisfying than running
scalding hot water over a poison ivy
rash, I certainly haven't found it.

Toilet seats are like slip-n-slides when you're really sweaty.

Things I struggle with: with a great tush like mine, why do the cops get called whenever I decide to proudly show it to the world? Sure, they were nuns, but still…

If I could save time in a bottle, the first thing I'd do is become a black market time merchant, selling low-grade time to temporal addicts.

You can have that Mexican kid…
Joss Whedon is my copilot.

Dear Insomnia: You are a prick. - Hatefully, me.

Man, I wish I was a 9th level elven thief / 11th level fighter with a Vorpal Sword and a Bag Of Holding.

Someday I will be cool enough
to own and wear a zoot suit.

Going to pitch a new reality TV show this fall called Fat Dudes Who Almost Have A Stroke Changing A Tire in 95 Degree Weather. #Just1Episode

We all do what we can, when we can... and then, most times, even that isn't enough to change our paths.

I'm thinking that either Meryl Streep, Jackie Chan, or Jamie Foxx would be perfect to play me in the story of my life.

I can finally add a new skill to my resume! As of today, I can tie a cherry stem into a knot with my tongue. So, yeah, I have that going for me, ladies.

I'm pretty sure in a previous life I was a one-legged burlesque dancer. It's the only thing that explains my fear of pairs of garter belts.

Today's Mantra: Dear all-powerful, transdimensional, invisible, and quirky supreme being, please give me the strength not to choke the ever living shit out of stupid people today. No matter how fun it would be. Thank you.

Why does the Breakfast of Champions inevitably lead to the Defecation of the Criminally Insane? #LifesGreatQuestions

My name? I go by many names. None of which you're worthy of pronouncing.

Dear Insomnia: The only way I'd ever appreciate you is if you were cuddly and a good kisser. As it stands, you're a stoned bum who is sleeping and peeing in the corner rather than cuddling with me.

There are days I wish I was Tigger. That sunnofa b!tch can bounce back from just about anything.

Dirty things heard on the Saturday cooking show: "Then, we're gonna top it with a vanilla sauce."

Things I Am (NOT) Thankful For (#06): Being this Pretty. You think you've got it bad? You have no idea how difficult it is being as gorgeous as I am. Answering fan mail, signing autographs on boobs, being constantly asked to be the future father of smitten women's to-be-conceived children, the stalkers, the periodic calls from celebrities asking for beauty secrets, dodging thrown panties and bras, the photo shoots, God calling and apologizing for breaking my mold... these are just the tip of the iceberg. Being this pretty is a lot of hard, thankless work. You want something to put on your Things To Be Thankful For list? Just praise the Maker that you aren't as pretty as me.

We have a new cat in the household.
I'm lobbying for the name "Pussy
Galore" but am encountering resistance
from the family. Maybe they will
be more open to "Octo-Pussy."

I have had "Eye of the Tiger"
stuck in my head all day. Strangely,
no pressing desire to run up stairs
or to punch butchered cows.

I have it on very good authority
that everybody poops. I think
I read it somewhere.

I'm pretty sure my "evil" mirror universe counterpart is an ice cream vendor from Hoboken... without a goatee but with impressive muttonchops and a HelloKitty! tattoo.

When I grow up, I want to be Yogi the Bear. Your pick-a-nick baskets will all be mine.

Is it still Mexican food if it's cooked by a Scotsman and served by a Korean girl?

When I erase a word, am I sending it via wormhole to another dimension?

Good morning all my good peeps! I hope your weekend has started in über groovy mode and will culminate in the pinnacle of awesome.

What's worst than being woken at 2:30 in the morning by insomnia? Nothing. Nothing is worse.

These things are nothing that advanced cloning technology and full memory duplication wouldn't solve.

If I had a unibrow, I would name it "Mr. Jiggly." That way, if anyone stared, I would just yell: Stop caressing Mr. Jiggly with your eyes!!!

My mantra for today: "Lord, give me the strength and willpower not to unleash my holy can of extreme whoopass on the stupid of the world."

First order of business on this brave new day: replace my blood with high-octane coffee.

Thinking about becoming a life coach for the criminally insane. Most of those folks aren't living up to their full artistic potential.

I'm almost positive there is a rabid clown under my bed… or a couple cats… pretty much a toss-up.

Whoever let loose ninja goats into my dream last night, screw you. You ruined a perfectly good top-secret mission I was on with Celine Dion.

Decisions, decisions. Do I go to work naked or dress somewhat professionally. Also, is body paint considered professional?

Today puts you one day closer to being my loyal servant. Bask in your freedom while you can.

That awkward moment when you are driving along and accidentally run over an entire cross country team, a power-walking club, 4 jaywalkers, and a pack of wild turkeys.

Fate and circumstances are both unrelenting, nagging, f*cking b!tches.

I've got Dolly Parton on a loop in my head today. Literally. She's jogging around my mental running track in a silk gym outfit.

My birthday: Today is the only day of the year when I like cake and spankings. The rest of the year you can keep your cake.

When I grow up, I want to cultivate a healthy sense of childlike wonder.

It's funny that after all these years the wifester is surprised when I get all excited about a movie marathon on TV… showing movies I already own on DVD or Blu-Ray.

Off to bed, finally. On tonight's dream agenda: miniaturizing myself to 1/4 inch like Ant Man and infiltrating the local sorority house. Aww yeah.

Good morning, everyone! I hope your day is full of hope and sugary, happy gumdrops. Except you, Monday. You can go screw yourself, you evil bastard.

Life should have more danger in it. For example, 1 in 2000 rolls of toilet paper should be moderately explosive if exposed to "processed" Mexican food.

When I become a superhero, I'm going to go by the alias of Dung Beetle! My catchphrase can be "Flinging the poo of freedom!"

This is one of those days I wish I were an anthropomorphic cat.

Do they still require airline passengers to wear pants? Asking for a friend.

Warning: The large mint in the urinal does NOT taste as good as it smells.

Welcome to [your workplace]. Please leave your name, your desire for quality work, and your soul at the door. Here's your number and your 6x6 cubicle. Next.

Happens every time I lay down. #HumanCatBed

There are days I seriously consider becoming a monk just so I don't have to hear the endless prattle of idiots.

It's that time of the year again when folks start wrapping their sweater puppies under layers of clothes. Poor constricted and smothered sweater puppies. #Winter

Now you know… and knowing is half the battle. The other half is superior numbers, advanced technology, and the willingness to fight dirty.

I have the best booty of all the
middle-aged, fat, bald guys I know.

Chloroform: works quicker on
me than sleeping pills.

Does everyone else get
tired of being tired?

The cake is a lie and the potato is a b!tch.

It feels like I've been waiting
for Friday my entire life.

Burning the candle at both
ends is for wimps. I just toss the
f*cking thing in the fire.

The only good thing about the
government shutdown and the impending
dystopia, societal collapse, and the
inevitable food riots is that I can live
off my own body fat for at least a year
before I have to resort to cannibalism.

I really need an entourage. I'm thinking blind Shaolin monks in leather jackets. Yeah, that'd be cool.

Heading off to dreamland for some interstellar exploration. Much better than your lame dreams of going to school/work without pants on.

May poo-flinging monkeys be the primary demographic of the studio audience watching the tragic sitcom that is your life.

Things I Am (NOT) Thankful For (#07): Getting Older. Ok, so this one just plain isn't fair. I bust my butt to gain a bunch of experience, skill, and mojo. And what happens? I start getting older. Where's the prize at the end of all that hard work? Grey hair? Bad back? F*ck that! I want my mansion, my millions, and my damn pony! Can't a grown man get a damn pony?

From the immortal words of Dr. Pond, therapist to the stars: "If your date brings candles, chloroform, duct tape, feathers, an ice pick, and a 12v battery on your weekend getaway, pick your safe word before leaving. Mine is 'cabbage'."

Is porn technically Saturday morning cartoons for adults?

Do toasters crave starting their day with electric toast?

When I grow up, I really want to be a monkey's uncle.

Is it just me, or is there a complete lack of one-legged, chain-smoking, German granny porn on Facebook? #EarlyMorningPhilosophy

I'm pretty sure a homeless clown snuck into my room last night and took a dump in my mouth. #DrinkingDues

Secret Agent Coffee: your mission, should you chose to accept it, is to wake my ass up.

That really bad taste in your mouth when you just woke up? Yeah, that was just Monday taking a crap on your dreams. Good morning.

Some days make you feel like you were kicked in the jiggly bits. Some days, getting kicked in the jiggly bits would be preferred to actually facing the day.

I'm thinking about starting a retro 80s No Hair Band.

I'm trying to be a leaf on the wind today; but all I can manage is emulating a brick in the dryer.

For everyone's reference: apparently it is illegal to open your door naked when a group of nuns stop by to teach you the holy word. The good news: 9 out of 10 nuns love the Full Pondy (if the cheers and catcalls are any indication). The bad news: Sister Mary Margarette O'Hennessy is a b!tch (and she apparently has the cops on speed dial).

Factoid. Now that's a funny word. Kind of like if a hemorrhoid had a baby with a dictionary.

I sense a disturbance in the sleep patterns… as if suddenly a million of my brain cells screamed out in unison, "Let's party, chubby dude! To hell with sleep!"

Oh, the strange looks you get when you walk into the grocery store naked.

For Halloween this year, I'm going as "unassuming guy who hands out candy while checking out the trick-or-treaters' moms."

Today is one of those days when I wish punching someone in the throat was an accepted response to them being an ass.

Some days, it's just not worth the effort to try to hide or dispose of the bodies. #SerialMurdererWorkStress

I'm considering getting a full body tattoo of a skinny person.

If I were having any more fun, I would actually be having fun.

There just aren't enough movies featuring elite French sheep commando units.

Had a dream I was exploring an abandoned hotel naked, avoiding robot sentries. Then I woke in the hotel lobby, surrounded by interested spectators. Sleepwalking on business trips sucks.

If anybody needs me, I'll be locked in an epic fight to the ignominious death with my arch-enemy, Boredom.

The amount of bullshit "data" being passed around as "fact" by sheeple is just f*cking astounding.

Bare-Assed Naked In Sp

By Chester B. Feelmebewbs
(Scientific Journal Reporter)

Some dreams never die, no matter how improbable.

What started out as a joke and a alcohol-fueled discussion at Balticon 48—the Maryland Regional Science Fiction and Fantasy Convention—finally became a reality yesterday, on September 23, 2018.

Mars now has its first nudist colony.

At 7:38 AM Eastern Standard Time, 28 men and 34 women—in groups of four—began entering the airlock of the Bare Minerals Nudist Warren (BMNW) in northern Elysium Planitia.

"When Paul E. Cooley (yes, THAT Paul Cooley) and I initially talked about the logistics of a nudie colony on another planet," said Scott Pond, the colony leader, "we never considered it had any real possibility. I mean, come on, who would ever back that kind of crazy, f*cked up idea. He or she would have to be a total nut-case."

That nutcase in question turned out to be billionaire author and philanthopist David Sobkowiak (the inventor of Boogs, the best-selling auto nose-picking finger extensions) and noted fan of nude people everywhere, Scott Roche (the inventor of the world's first working x-ray glasses.

Both Roche and Sobkowiak designed and funded the remote construction of the BMNW facility a full three years before the first humans actually set foot in the 253 thousand square foot multi-level martian resort. The entire facility is powered by the extensive solar farm generated across the plains to the south of the temperature-regulated habitat. Designed to perpetualy be at a balmy 78 degrees

Pond rep
powder in
inch. He c

Tori's fi
little chilly
first orgas
descendin

"It's a v
with the s
said. "It a
a harsh

Why is it that when women fart it's cute, but when I fart I get the "holy crap my eyes are literally melting" comments? Double standard?

When I grow up, I want to be the astronaut who leads the mission to form the first nude Mars colony.

I have the soul of an explorer, the heart of a lion, and the body of a bowl of Jell-O.

U2 has their "Sunday Bloody Sunday."
I have my "Monday F*cking Monday."

Please give me the strength to do what I must today and to have the will not to slap the crap out of anyone, no matter how much they may deserve it. #TheyReallyDeserveIt #PondysSerenityPrayer

It's so difficult to wake up looking this pretty.

Some days it's just not worth climbing the tree to peek in the neighbors' window.

Today's headache is brought to you by a rusty number 3 railroad spike driven directly through my temples.

I want to start a fortune cookie company that only gives snarky fortunes, like: "You know nothing," "Only idiots read fortune cookies," and "You're fat, go home." You know, inspirational fortunes.

Bought a frozen turkey today.
Just not sure if it's a regular one
or one of the jive variety.

I'd work harder at stealing all of your souls, but frankly, most of them aren't worth the effort. #DaemonProblems

If I win the lottery, I swear I won't be obnoxious. Heck, I probably wouldn't talk to most of you ever again for that matter, so it's not as though you would know if I was being obnoxious.

When I grow up, I want to be an angry despot with a predilection for roasting my enemies in superheated beef gravy.

Must. Make. Coffee... Only. Cure. For. My. Narcoleptic. Malaise.

I swear: if I win the lottery, I'm so going to make a "Scott of New Hampshire" birthday-suit calendar. And then toss them out of airplanes over heavily populated areas. #YouAreWelcome

Can you make cheese out of freshly squeezed llama milk? I'm asking for a friend.

Feces: it's what *was* for dinner.

I tried to give a f*ck today, but I couldn't even bother with a lascivious catcall or a halfhearted grope. #EffingMondayHasRuinedMe

A rapper with a nose mining habit: Sir-Picks-And-Flicks-Alot.

I really want to turn my head and cough when the TSA agent rams his hand up my crotch in the search for the gummy bears I typically warm in my boxers. But I fear they might keep me grounded. Or worse, ask me for some. No one gets any of my squishy, freshly-warmed, gummy bears. No One.

I wish I had an outrageous accent, huh huh wee wee.

I'd be a fantastic benevolent dictator.

Consider not why the laundry basket is empty. Instead, realize that its state of fullness or emptiness matters not in light of the discarded clothes on the floor.

I'm pretty sure in a previous life I was a chamber pot, and my karma ensures I'm still dealing with shit.

Things I Am (NOT) Thankful For (#08): Ice cube toes. Seriously, I think my toes could freeze water at this point.

Everything tastes better with gravy.

I swear, when I win the lottery, I promise I will only be obnoxious and unbearable for a day. Two at most. Okay, maybe 4,000 days.

Dear Abby: I'd love to lose weight but I'm afraid I'll lose my awesome cleavage and won't be as attractive or as bouncy on the treadmill. –Scott

The moral and sexual ambiguity of earthworms and dryer lint is disheartening.

I suspect that Colonel Sanders has very little practical combat experience.

One thing that could make today better would be a Milli Vanilli concert.

If I was a gynecologist, I would make it a point to recommend new hairstyles to every client and offer tic tacs after the exam just to make the patient wonder.

The best part of Christmas? Santa always leaves us one of his elves who aren't as productive anymore. Nothing quite like roast elf and gravy.

I want my tombstone to read "was buried with a lot of gold" and I want my burial suit to be made of gold lamé. #StupidGraveRobbers #Suckers

Apparently, I am Monday's prison b!tch.

I would be a fantastic hermit. I could even be the Leader of All Hermits. I wonder if Hermits have meetings to establish pecking order.

I just found a roll of dollar bills in my PJ bottoms pocket. I really don't know what to think of this.

I would say it's as cold as a snow witch's teat while playing ice volleyball in the nude, but I think her nip would actually be warmer. #Minus25WindChill

Biggs Darklighter had an awesome 70's porn 'stache.

Life is like a crossword puzzle created by roving bands of blind, typewriting chimpanzees.

There are no original thoughts in this universe, just recycled snippets of mental doggerel.

What is the best way to serve house cat for dinner? I'm asking for a friend.

I just threw a pair of socks into the clothes basket. At the same time. From 10 ft. away. This reaffirms that I am a god. Tremble, mere mortals, for my reign will be harsh.

Going to my happy place in my mind. Strangely enough, that place is stocked with cheerleaders, whips, mounds of chocolate, and heavy metal music.

Who do you think would win in an all you can eat contest: Hannibal Lector, Leatherface, or Jeffrey Dahmer?

I wish I had octopus testicles instead of arms. Oh, wait, I may have misspelled that.

Chicken slaughtered, fondled, diced, spiced, and cooked for the week. Eat your black heart out, Julia Childs.

You know what there's not enough of? Pictures of monkeys smoking cigars and riding unicycles.

I wish I had a trained pet miniature porcupine. I would totally use him as a reloadable hand grenade. And I would call him George.

Terence Trent D'Arby should start an Etsy store for hand-crafted miniature ceramic wishing wells.

My imaginary friend just said he doesn't believe in me. #Paradox

I'd like to say I'm kicking Monday's
ass and taking names, but that's
just escapism as it has its way with
me while I bite the pillow.

Insomnia has a way of making one
ponder the relevancy of the bullshit
that seems to take up much of our
lives. What is the point, really?

I am a huge fan of the Oxford Comma,
em dashes, en dashes, and semicolons; plus
other forms of down-trodden punctuation.

Jack Frost is nipping at my toes. Not for long. I'm putting a stop to that little bastard once I find my baseball bat.

Coffee is the Sweat of the Gods. I guess I'm a freaking weirdo for drinking God Sweat™. Don't be a hater.

What would the genetic, biological, fashion, and social ramifications be if monkeys could indeed fly from your butt? Discuss.

Who the heck stole my weekend? Give it back and I promise I won't call the cops. I have other ways of making you pay.

You know what's funny? Angry self-entitled airline passengers who don't understand the difference between boarding time and takeoff time; and also don't realize the cabin door needs to close between those two times.

Not saying that all of you are mindless drones, but how the hell can you watch this drivel? *stares in horror at the TV*

Didn't George Washington cross the Amazon in a prop plane? #NoSenseOfHistoricalPerspective

I would never f*ck an alpaca... but I do support the alpaca's right to love whoever they desire. #Equality

You know, it's not easy to drive 90 miles an hour in a residential zone full of trick-or-treaters and still be able to text properly without spelling errors. Especially when you are driving blindfolded. While listening to Rick Astley.

Remember kids: naked hugs, not drugs. This PSA brought to you by Trojan Brand condoms and the Census Bureau.

I really want a small armored battle monkey... one that will kneecap all my enemies and fling poo at them. I would call him George.

When you are feeling down in the dumps, don't worry: not everyone can be as gorgeous as I am. Remember: You have a great personality.

You know what there's not enough of? Cross-species square dancing. I mean, come on. How cute would a monkey and a cat doing a dos-à-dos be?

I'm all for hearing the voice of the people, but why does it have to be so negative and ill-informed?

Monkeys: the other other other other other other white meat.

That moment when you wake after a ninja nap session in terror because you don't know where or who you are. #DroolingHorror

Another day of fun and festivities. And by "fun and festivities," I of course mean "abject boredom and ripping out one's hair in stressful frustration."

And yet, despite my own protests and prayers (not to mention bribes), Monday has arrived again. #PowerlessToStopIt

I have an overpowering desire to go into politics and to put a bunch of silly rules into law. Just like the other politicians. #PeerPressure #AllTheNotCoolKidsAreDoingIt

BREAKING NEWS: Cats are jerks. Science says so. Science!

RELATED NEWS: Cats tossed out of fourth story windows do not fly very well. Nor do they bounce. Much.

You ever get so burned out from the daily grind and people that you'd actually look forward to a pandemic to force some necessary sanity and genetic culling?

I wonder: If I stole someone's soul, would I get his or her extra hours each day? I could totally use them.

I don't always have insomnia, but when I do, it wakes me from a blissful sleep.

Things I Am (NOT) Thankful For (#09): BOOBIES. Just joking... those are on my list of Things That Make Life Bearable. That, and Mint Chocolate Chip Ice Cream... Yum. However, let's make this one The Assholes Who Contributed To The Poor Body-Image That Some Women Have Who Are Self-Conscious About <Insert Body Part Here>. If you are a wonderful, caring, friendly person, those little body differences just plain don't matter. Tall, short, skinny, fat, long hair, short hair, no hair, big/small/missing/lop-sided boobs, extra finger or nipple, big butt, no butt, extra butt, mustache, 70s boosh, delicate frame, built like a fire hydrant, or any other variation... none of that matters if you are a quality individual. Any jackass who tells you otherwise is a fool. Men who are worthwhile will love you for being you, not judge you for some unimportant body quirk. Don't give the assholes the power over who you are. Be you and be free to be you no matter what. Also, call me.

If I could marry non-living things,
I would totally present you with the future Mrs. Hot-Cup-of-Coffee Pond.

I'd do my normal "Monday" rant here, but even I don't have adequate words or energy.

There is something I must tell you: I am not left-handed. #ForShame

You know what I love about flying? Getting to my destination. Oh, and the free gratuitous lap dances from the drunk pilot and stoned navigator. Can't forget that.

I want to start a protest group, just not sure about the topic. Maybe Portabello mushrooms. #SlimyBastardFungus

The arterial buildup in my heart just shattered in ecstasy.

When someone finally gets around to starting a Wikipedia page about me, remember: I once wrestled an octopus while wearing a speedo. #TrueStory #OrIsIt #TrueEnoughForWikipedia

Remember that scene in that one movie where that actor playing that one character that said that thing while doing that other thing?

This whole morning thing is for the birds. And I don't even like worms.

Bewbs. Now that I have your attention, I'd like to talk about my Mexican yard savior, Jesus. Have you taken Jesus Martinez into your life for landscaping opportunities?

Dear celestial power in charge of delivering migraines to good boys and girls: go to hell and take your "gift" with you.

Nothing quite like the delicate sounds of your youngest child vomiting all over her bedroom wall at 3:30AM to herald in another delightful Monday.

I'd make my life story into a movie, but it would be so tough to find an actor with as much technical, geeky, outdoorsy, friendly, and pure presence as me.

What if something actually HAD crawled up there and died? Maybe a favorite small pet? You wouldn't pick on them about their fart stink then, would you?

It is so hard being this pretty.

Goodnight kiddies. Make sure you wash behind your ears and brush your teeth. Oh, and no need to look under your beds. Really, there's no monsters under here. Really.

Today's safe word is "porcupine."

I'm easy, easy like Sunday morning.
But not as easy as some insatiable
days that we all know.
*Yes, Friday, I'm looking at you, you
gigolo-tramp. Keep your milky full moon
and your sunbeam in your pants*

Take the wheel, Jesús... I gotta reload my
beer koozie. #MyGardenerIsMyCoPilot

I've decided that randomly
deciding to do random things is
f*cking random and stupid.

I'm considering getting a rabbit because I prefer my end-of-the-world emergency rations to be fresh.

Whenever I encounter a family in the airport talking a foreign language, I always imagine they are talking about how groovy my mustache is.

Today would be a great day to be possessed by a vengeful Sumerian God hell-bent on decimating all humanity.

Thinking about starting my own religion. Should the deity be a humanoid male, a humanoid female, or a lusty androgynous tentacle beast with a heart of gold?

Remember: Soylent Green is people. Therefore people are stale, dry, a little crunchy, and full of artificial flavors.

Man, eating sushi is like eating raw fish that hasn't been cooked.

Note to self: stop giving yourself notes to remind yourself to do things you'll never do anyway.

We all need something magical to believe in, to get us through the day. Me, I believe there are bacon and Cadbury Egg trees just waiting to be discovered.

Dear weekend: if you decided to appear in the next 5 minutes to take me away from all this, I wouldn't fight you or resist. Honest.

Lucky Charms has never brought me any sort of luck. #Misleading

Your task for the evening: use the phrase "amorous moose" in a sentence. Go!

And on the Tenth day, God made me a steak burrito... and it was good.

Time to drag myself outta bed. This day isn't going to get going without me. Oh, wait... the day doesn't give a crap about me and will carry on without my foolhardy attempts to help it along. I'm going back to sleep.

My weight is just right for my height.
#SaysTheFatManOnStilts

Never bite the hand that feeds you. Unless it is made from chocolate, then always bite the chocolate hand that feeds you.

You may not be able to lick your own elbow, but you definitely can lick the elbow of a stranger on the subway. Once.

My best advice? Don't.
When in doubt, just don't.
Applies to about everything: careers, fashion, going commando, dating Charlie Sheen, etc.

Today's Important PSA: Never urinate on or above a live electrical outlet. You're welcome.

Thank Dog for spell chuck.

If loving me is wrong, you don't want to be right.

Boner Wave is the name of my Amish Pop cover group.

I deserve an 80s montage today. Stat!

It's ok to think I'm awesome... 8 out of 10 people polled secretly think I'm yummy. 2 out of 10 are in denial. Remember folks, numbers don't lie... it's people using numbers who lie.

Why do #AmWriting when you could be doing #AmWritingNaked #WhileEatingABagOfCheetos?

I would make a fantastic Spiderman, if Spiderman was a bald fat dude who's afraid of heights, spiders, and clowns.

Things I Am (Not) Thankful For (#10): Scratchy Toilet Paper. Man, what a pain in the ass.

I would make a great Iron Man as well, if the armor was made out of spandex.

I would also make a very sexy Wonder Woman or Ms. Marvel. I certainly have the bodacious ass and moobs for it. #HairyMoobs

Good morning, my peeps! May your day ooze with the awesome of a fantastic attitude and not the ick of past mistakes.

Dear Insomnia Faeries: Take your magical AwakeAllNight™ dust and sprinkle it on someone else.

When one door closes, another opens. Gotta love being a cat burglar.

Amazing that while in the 20th and 21st centuries as science, information exchange, and comfort levels advanced, etiquette and manners of society eroded. #Coincidence?

Tell me this: what is the current administration doing about the looming threat of the #MolePeople?!? Huh? Well?

I'd probably make a passable middle-aged Wolverine, though I'm not putting that nasty cigar in my mouth. #PhallicNonstarter

In light of all the drama oozing through social media today, I have this to say: I like lemon cupcakes and they'll never take that from me.

Forcing a creative idea is like trying to force out a fart. You never know whether it's going to be great or if you'll end up with a pile of crap in your hand.

I love flying. It's just the smell of unwashed jackasses that puts me off a bit.

There aren't enough brilliantly diabolical plans in the world. Some evil genius needs to rectify that.

My happy thought of the day: I've still got the body of Adonis somewhere under all this fat.

When I grow up, I want to be a sassy, foul-mouthed—but lovable—Asian grannie.

43.57% of the statistics used in polls and statistics-based explanations are fallacious, mired in ambiguity, derived from questionable sources and demographically stratified selection criteria, and are often just made-up on the spot to suit the desires of statisticians.

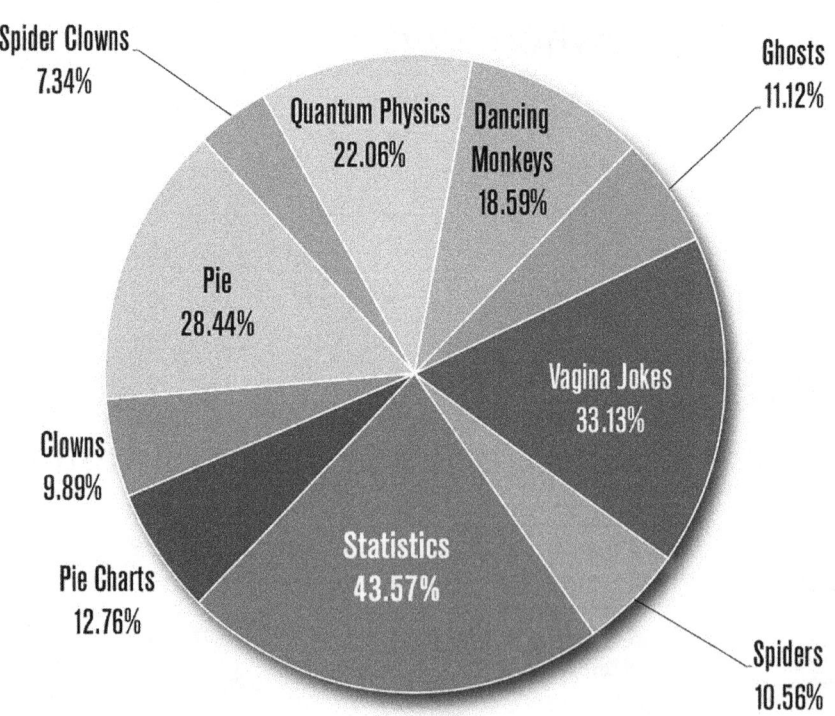

Just ran full tilt at the back of my closet. No Narnia there but apparently there are stars.

<grumble> <grumble> morning <grumble> <grumble>

Bacon. (Sorry for sultry talk)

To hell with sexy, I'm bringing angry back.

I have learned the hard way that the hard way of learning is hard.

I really wish I had a battle rhino. I would call him George.

People, man… people.
#TasteLikeChicken

It's 12:15AM and I'm bored. I figure I have three choices: 1) pick a random person on social media to have a fight with about a topic I have no clue about, 2) find random pictures of ninja kittens, or 3) post a strange list of three choices.

Creatives must create. That's the fifth law of thermodynamics, I think.

Dammit Jim, I'm a doctor, not a flamingo dancer with a bad hip.

I'm at that point in my life story where the mysterious benefactor appears and offers me tons of money for completing a wacky quest. #StillWaiting #HurryUp

"Get your toe out of your mouth."
#NeverThought
#HaveToSayToYour8YearOld

Coffee coffee coffee coffee coffee…

It's easy to convince people you've done nothing good. It's tougher to convince them you've done nothing wrong.

There just aren't enough Barbra Streisand speed metal cover bands.

Siri isn't much of a conversationalist.

You too can dramatically change someone's life today. All it takes is for you to buy an awesome cup of coffee and give it to me. Believe me, it would change my day and I promise to be very dramatic about it. I'll even play a Sarah McLachlan song to commemorate the event. I may even shed a tear.

Happy Friday the 13th. May your terror level be exquisite and horrible.

Look, I'm wearing a belly shirt! Oh, wait.... *pulls shirt back down* ...never mind.

Finally wearing pants. Damn you, Responsibility, for making me do things I don't want to do.

Did you ever know that you're my gyro? #BetteMidlerFoodSongs

Goodnight, sweet Prince. Please, don't wake me up with your songs about colorful rain, red cars, or fruity hats.

What if Harry Potter had actually been born Mary Potter instead? Discuss.

The sleep, it calls to me. Much like the voices that tell me to dance in my underwear during a thunderstorm, yet different.

It's unfortunate that this much awesome
and badassery could end up in such
a hottie as me (instead of in you).

If I can get even one person to
call me a "Magnificent Bastard,"
then it's a good day.

The voices in my head have
completely stopped making sense. I
fear they might be losing it here.

Don't even get me started on Barbie's "boyfriend" Ken, or his "friend" Jacques. Talk about living a lie. Open your eyes, Barbie. Own it Ken: be proud.

This is either the tenderest diced steak I've cooked or I accidentally warmed up a can of dog food again.

If I ever get raised to be the supreme celestial leader of a church, I vow this: at least once a month will be "Mass in the Holy Buff." You are welcome.

The Sacred Burning Liquid of
Martyr Jose Cuervo shall be
my holiest of sacraments.

There is no such thing as TMI, people!
We live in the information age; the
more of, it the better. In related news,
I'm naked and may have "accidentally"
smeared peanut butter all over myself.

I would've made a fantastic boy toy
to someone with really poor vision
and a really large bank account.

Ignorance is Bliss. And Bliss needs some help in the grammar department.

I want a giant armored warthog that I can ride into battle. I would call him George.

OH from one of the voices in my head to another: I'd need a tractor-trailer of TP to clean up the shitty day he's had.

I hope Santa doesn't wake me up this year to try to give me reindeer kisses. That dude's mustache tickles and he smells like sugar cookies and peppermint.

Well, it's Monday again. I wonder whose hopes and dreams will be crushed today? #PleaseNotMe

Follow your dreams. Unless your dreams tell you that pink elephants can fly and shoot lasers from their eyes. Don't trust those dreams.

Why yes, I AM a foxy gentleman.

In my next life, I want to
be a cyborg ostrich.

Tastes like chicken.

I have been mentally dressing you in my
mind all day. Please wear more clothing.

Only real men can braid their chest hair into macramé art.

Things I Am (Not) Thankful For (#11): People who don't understand what is best in life. You see this especially around the holidays. When asked what they are thankful for and what is best in life, you typically see wishy-washy answers like friends, family, their health, their children, etc. etc. etc. Bleah. They think they know what is best in life? "Wrong!" "What is best in life?" "To crush your enemies, see them driven before you, and to hear the lamentation of their women." "That is good! That is good." You all have a thing or three to learn from the barbarian king.

Remember: WWCRD - What would Casey Ryback Do?

Some days it's not even worth trying to come up with an elaborate plan for world domination.

If I were a Transformer, my vehicle shape would probably be a ghetto El Camino with fuzzy dice. What would yours be?

I bet Mrs. Claus smokes menthol cigars. Probably has a mistletoe tattoo around her belly button as well. And a tramp-stamp that proudly proclaims, "my cookie is tastier and lower in calories... want a nibble?"

I'm pleased to announce that I'm the ambassador for all fat white bald dudes everywhere. It was just announced on the Fat White Bald Dude Inspirational Network.

Life is like a box of chocolates. Chocolates that have been eaten by ants. And that are kind of old and crusty from being in the sun too long.

I want to create a coffee table book called "The Big Ass Book of Random Pictures With Unrelated Quotes."

Nothing quite like a 13-hour workday to put hair on your chest, make you irresistible to women, and bring about world peace. Though it doesn't seem to be working for me.

They say breakfast is the most important meal of the day. That's why I start out every day by drinking the blood of my enemies.

Coffee injection acquired. Resume normal operations in 3... 2... 1...

Oh, hello Insomnia. We meet again. And I see you've bought a friend. What's his name? Heartburn? Just freaking fantastic. Well you're both here, so come on in.

I'm only going to say this once: all of you need to stop showing up unannounced in my action-adventure dreams as secondary characters. I really don't believe any of you are actually CIA Chiefs, evil proctologists, my extremely amorous step-aunt Gertrude, or Spanish-speaking visitors from Alpha Centauri. If you must make a guest appearance, be believable... and at least bring beer.

Is there a cheat code for this Monday thing? I'm not really interested in this chapter, so I'd like to skip past it. Can we get to the part where I save the day? #IfTheWeekWereAVideoGame

I feel a disturbance... as if millions of unique individual snowflakes suddenly cried out in terror... and were silenced. *sprinkles more rock-salt on the driveway*

I exercise vicariously through other people's vigorous workouts. #Science!

Remember Folks: today is National Go-To-Work-Commando Day™. *Also known as "I should have done more laundry this week" Day.

I've heard a rumor that you like big butts and that you cannot lie.

I'm thinking about getting a hairless cat with a full body tattoo of a regular cat.

And what happens next clogs the sewer for miles around. Click here to see more! #TacoTuesdays

Be yourself... because it is so difficult to take on the genetic traits and DNA sequences of someone else.

I'm shocked that despite kiwis having fur, they don't taste like meat.

Life is a highway. And I'm going to drive it like I'm an arthritic 105-year-old granny with severe cataracts. All night long.

Mental Graffiti **219**

Don't hate me because I'm beautiful. But go ahead and hate me for being such a charming Muthah F*cker.

No matter how much makeup and lipstick you put on, Monday, I know it's really you. Don't try to masquerade as Tuesday.

I wonder if there is a Photoshop filter I can apply to my life to give it that funky low-light feel.

There just aren't enough freeze-dried giant feces-art sculptures of famous people.

My pillow totally understands me. On the other hand, my blanket is an asshole. This pretty much sums up my existence.

I think I lose 20 IQ points every time I attend a corporate meeting. I'm currently at -239,674 IQ points.

There are days when I wish I had a real invisibility cloak, vorpal sword, and bag of holding. If I had those, I could have totally kicked today's butt. #EffingMonday

Making a big life change is scary. But you know what is even scarier? Spider clowns.

The next time you get upset about where life is taking you, remember this: bacon.

If loving cheese is wrong, I don't want to be right.

Don't be duped by the poultry industry. It doesn't taste like chicken. It tastes like people. PEOPLE! EVERYTHING TASTES LIKE PEOPLE!!!!

Please, please let tonight's dream be a flying dream. I'm not sure I can handle the bloodthirsty broccoli mutants again. Damn evil veggies.

When they make the biopic of my inglorious life, I hope they have John Travolta narrate it in the voice of Vinnie Barbarino, while dressed as the mom from "Hairspray."

If I were any more charming you'd all call me Prince.

If you can't be happy, at least be obnoxious.

It's days like this that I consider:
if I had feathers, what pattern
of plumage would I prefer?

Morning benediction: may you survive
the (un)necessary evils of this day with
minimal tears, scars, and bruising.

I wish I could get myself cloned,
but I fear the world would implode
from that much awesome.

OH (from one of the voices in my head): there aren't enough ninja monkeys to battle that level of stupid.

Welcome to yet another Monday. I hope it is gentle with you. Or that you black out from the pain.

OH (from the voices in my head): there isn't enough toilet paper in the entire northeast to clean up the amount of bullsh!t spewing from your mouth, son.

"I wonder if monkeys can be trained to hang-glide?" and other insomnia-induced musings.

Remember folks: it's all fun and games until you shatter your pelvis.

My goal in life is to be able to walk down the street and have people whisper to each other, "Damn, that dude has an ass that just won't quit."

With enough of a perspective shift, just about any statement can be viewed as being gender, sexually, or racially biased. Discuss.

When harvesting organs from "volunteers," make sure you pick the hotel room on the end and bring a ball gag.

And on the 9th day, God made a Long Island Iced Tea and just chilled. And it was good.

Is eating donut holes considered to be culinary sodomy of a donut?

I'm pretty sure that I am a grapefruit trapped in a chocolate glazed-donut's body.

They have only the finest intellectually-challenged individuals working at the donut shop today.

Spicy Balloon Knot is the name of my Mexican siesta cover band.

"I am the mother f*cking Laundry King!"
-Samuel L. Jackson, doing chores

You know what? For being just figments of my imagination, y'all are all right in my book. I'm glad I thought you up. Now go the f*ck away. I'm done with you.

I was really hoping this would end with a "your mom" joke.

Do you want to hear news and get an email when Scott publishes a new book or has a new project being released? Go to his website and sign up for Scott's newsletter today!

Visit and subscribe: **http://scottpond.com/**

The only time you'll receive emails is when he has new published books or new projects being released (and no more frequently than once a month!).

Also, you will not get spammed!

He doesn't even like spam... too much sodium.

An artist, graphic designer, humorist, photographer, and writer from Charlottesville, Virginia, Scott E. Pond has his hands in so many creative outlets and projects that it's surprising he can even sleep some days.

Honestly, most days he doesn't.

His designs have been seen gracing the books of: New York Times Bestselling author Scott Sigler; Parsec Award winning author Paul E. Cooley; award winning novelist and screenwriter Matt Wallace; prolific author Jake Bible; Sue Baiman; M. Jandreau; Doc Coleman, and many, many others.

Mental Graffiti is his first publication as an author.

For more information about current/upcoming projects, please visit **http://scottpond.com**

To subscribe to his newsletter, please visit **http://scottpond.com**

To stalk Scott on social media:
    Twitter: **https://twitter.com/ScottEPond**
    Facebook: **https://www.facebook.com/scottepond**
    Google+: **https://plus.google.com/+scottpond**

To contact Scott:
    Email: **scott@scottpond.com**

www.ingramcontent.com/pod-product-compliance
Lightning Source LLC
Chambersburg PA
CBHW061429040426
42450CB00007B/970